THEN AND THERE SERIES
GENERAL EDITOR
MARJORIE REEVES

The Rebecca Riots

CHRISTOPHER SCHENK

Illustrated from contemporary sources

LONGMAN

LONGMAN GROUP LIMITED
Longman House, Burnt Mill, Harlow, Essex CM20 2JE, UK
and Associated Companies throughout the World

First published 1985
ISBN 0 582 22171 4

Set in 11/12½ pt Linotron Baskerville
Produced by Longman Group (F.E.) Limited
Printed in Hong Kong

Er cof am Alcwyn Evans (1828–1902)
a Michael Bowen (1817–1854)

Acknowledgements

I have made considerable use of David Williams's book, *The Rebecca Riots* (University of Wales Press, 1955) with its extremely detailed foot-notes.

The staff of the Bodleian library, Oxford, and of the National Library of Wales, Aberystwyth, have, as always, been courteous and helpful.

Ruth Marris originally suggested the idea of writing this book to me.

My mother has given invaluable assistance with Welsh sources as well as encouragement and support throughout.

The publishers are grateful to the following for permission to reproduce photographs: Carmarthen Museum, pages 12, 36 (photo: Pete Davis); Dyfed Archive Service/Carmarthenshire Record Office and Mrs E. Barry, pages 33, 42; Mary Evans Picture Library, page 52; Illustrated London News Picture Library, 13; National Library of Wales, pages 6, 9, 27, 47; Punch, page 45; Welsh Folk Museum, page 21.
Cover: Rebecca and her daughters assembling to destroy a turnpike gate. A contemporary print. National Library of Wales.

Short extracts taken from: W. J. Lewis, 'The conditions of labour in mid-Cardiganshire in the early nineteenth-century', *Ceredigion*, iv, 1963 (page 22); Allwyn Evans, MS 12368E in the National Library of Wales (pages 28–30, 37, and 38–9); H. Tobit Evans, *Rebecca and her Daughters*, Educational Publishing Company, Cardiff 1910 (pages 30 and 46); *Tarian y Gweithiwr*, 4 November 1886, page 58.

Contents

Words printed in *italics* are explained in the Glossary on page 63.

To the Reader

The Rebecca riots took place nearly 150 years ago, in 1843, in a distant part of Wales: very different surroundings from present day riots. Young farmers dressed up in women's clothes and chopped down *toll gates* and set fire to *toll houses*. But although the Rebecca riots seem very different from today's riots, there are likenesses.

The riots were sparked off by the farmers refusing to pay tolls. These were the sums of money they had to pay when they took their carts or animals along the main roads. But the tolls were not the main cause of the riots. The riots took place because many people were out of work and many more did not have enough money. The ordinary people of *West Wales* felt that they were very different from the rich and powerful people. They spoke a different language and had a different form of religion from the people who made the laws. They felt they were unfairly treated by these people. When the rioting was at its worst there was really no law and order in West Wales at all. Policemen and soldiers had to stick together for safety, and most of the local people, young and old, were against them.

The Rebecca riots died down as quickly as they flared up. But in the years that followed, the story of Rebecca was told again and again in Wales. The story gave hope to people who were poor and oppressed by those set over them. It reminded them that poor people could stand up for their rights and that they could win at least a small victory over their oppressors. The story has not often been told in recent years, but it still has an important message for us and raises important questions. These questions can be asked about the riots of today just as much as they can be asked about the Rebecca riots: When, if ever, is it right to take the law into your own hands and turn to violence? How does it come about that an entire community turns against the police and the law? Is it right that there should be a big difference between the way the rich live and the way the poor live?

1 The Toll Gate

It is midnight. The sky is clear. The moon is full, lighting up the dirt road that winds its way along the side of the valley. There are few houses to be seen: one or two lonely farms on the hillside, a cluster of labourer's cottages in the far distance, and, next to the toll gate that is shut and bolted across the dirt road, there is the tiny dwelling place of the *toll keeper* and his family. They have long since gone to bed for there is no night traffic on this lonely Welsh road.

But the toll keeper is woken up from his sleep, for along the road a strange and unruly mob are coming towards the toll gate, shouting and banging drums as they come. Their leaders seem to be women – or at least they are dressed in women's clothes. The first three are riding horses, but even the horses are in disguise with white sheets draped over them, making them look like ghosts in the moonlight. When they arrive at the toll gate the leading rider dismounts. There is no doubt that he is a man, in spite of his petticoats and bonnet for he is almost bursting out of the women's clothes he has borrowed. He takes a stick from one of his followers and, pretending to be old and blind, hobbles to the gate.

'What is this, my children?' he asks in mock surprise. 'There is something in my way. I cannot go on.'

'What is it, mother Rebecca? Nothing should stand in your way,' answers a strong young man, also dressed in women's clothes.

'I do not know, my children. I am old and cannot see well.'

'Shall we come and move it out of your way, mother Rebecca?'

How a contemporary artist pictured Rebecca and her daughters attacking a toll gate

'Wait!' says 'Rebecca' feeling the gate with 'her' stick. 'It seems like a great gate put across the road to stop your old mother.'

'We will break it down, mother. Nothing should stand in your way.'

'But perhaps it will open,' says 'Rebecca' making a great show of feeling the locks and the bolts. 'Oh no, my dear children, it is bolted and locked. What is to be done?'

'It must be taken down, mother, because you and your children must get through.'

At this point the leader of the rioters stopped pretending that he was an old woman bent double over a stick. He stood up straight and, facing the crowd, he roared:

'Off with it then, my dear children. It has no business here.'

There were very nearly a hundred people who heard this command but it only needed twenty or so to chop down the toll gate with the hatchets they had brought with them. In less than ten minutes the gate and the gate posts were in pieces in the road.

Rioters acted out this sort of scene many times during 1843 at toll gates in various parts of Dyfed. They removed more than a hundred toll gates in this way and also pulled down a number of toll keeper's houses. The rioters were often disguised as women and the leader was always called Rebecca. Police and soldiers were sent for to stop these attacks but they never knew when or where Rebecca and her children would decide to pay a night time visit.

Nor could they discover who this mysterious 'lady' was, although there were all kinds of rumours about Rebecca. But there was no secret about who her children were. They were the farmers and farm labourers of West Wales who were angry because they had very little money. They had worked hard to grow crops only to find that they could not sell them for a good price. They had to pay money out to all sorts of people and they complained bitterly about it. The tolls that they had to pay out every time their wagons went along the road were the last straw. They met together at night to destroy toll gates, not because tolls were the worst of their grievances, but because the gates were easy to attack. Like many present day vandals, they destroyed whatever came to hand because they were not strong enough to attack the real causes of their troubles.

2 The Young Historian

At the time of the riots a boy called Alcwyn Evans was living in Carmarthen. He was fourteen years old and the son of a schoolteacher. We know quite a lot about him because when he grew up he wrote about the history of the place in which he lived. He filled many stoutly bound books with his neat handwriting, although sadly not one of them was ever printed. But they are kept in the National Library of Wales for people to read today.

Sometimes he wrote about things that happened a long time ago. At other times he wrote about events that had happened in his life time. In one book he tells the story of the Rebecca riots, using information from old newspapers but also remembering some of the things he had seen as a boy. For he was always interested in history – and history, after all, is happening all the time. He was always trying to find out what was going on by talking to people and asking questions. He wasn't just interested in what had happened. His favourite question was 'Why?'.

Carmarthen, the town where he lived, was considered large in those days, although only about 10,000 people lived there. But it was certainly the largest place for a long way round. It was a rough and violent town. Every time there was an election there would be fighting in the streets and several times there had been rioting when food was scarce. These riots were difficult to stop because the town only had about twelve policemen.

Many of the people in the town were poor and lived

crowded together in the back alleys. Sometimes as many as

four families lived in a house with only four rooms. Along the riverside there were many fishermen. In the fishing season they managed to make a living, but for the rest of the year they were often penniless. There were also a few people who made hats and some who knitted stockings. Many of the richer people were traders who did a lot of business with the farmers at the markets which were held several times a week.

On market days the farmers would come in from the country for miles around and the town would be crowded with people and sheep and cattle. The farmers were very different from the townspeople, although they were certainly no better off. They were more proud and more independent than the poor people of Carmarthen. These market days gave Alcwyn a good chance to find out what had been going on in the

A page from Alcwyn Evan's story of the Rebecca Riots

The Rising of the Welsh Rebeccaites

in their endeavour to free themselves from the injustice of the excessive tolls which the various Turnpike Trusts and their Lessees imposed on them. After demolishing the gates and bars, the Farmers turned their attention to the new Poor-Law, the alleged increase in the Commutation of Tithes apportionments, the Bastardy acts, &c. The name of Rebecca took rise from Genesis XXIV. 60. "And they blessed Rebekah, and said × × Be thou the mother of thousands of millions, and let thy seed possess the Gate of those which hate them". Isaiah. XLV. I. 2. "× × the gates shall not be shut, × × I will break in pieces the gates of Brass, and cut in sunder the Bars of iron."

EFEL-WEN.

1839 June 15th. Some time ago, handbills were fixed on many public doors at Efelwen, near Llandissilio. Co. Pembr. and in that neighbourhood stating where and when a meeting would be held to take into consideration the propriety of the Toll Gate fixed at Efelwen, &c. The Magistrates in the vicinity were told that it was generally expected that the concourse would proceed from the meeting to destroy the Toll Gate and House. Several special constables were sworn in, and sent to protect the piace. The evening, about a week ago, came the meeting was held, and immediately at its conclusion, about 400 men, some dressed in female garments, and others with blackened faces, marched to the toll-gate, huzza-ing for free laws, and free travelling to coal-pits &

lime-kilns. They drove the "specials" from their stations, and pursued them over the adjoining fields. Having done so they returned to the Gate, and in the course of three hours, the house was torn down to within a yard to the ground, the gate was shattered to pieces with large sledge hammers, and the gate posts were sawn off, and carried away. The Whitland Trust had listened to Thomas Bullen, the lessee, and had decidedly mismanaged affairs by placing Gates and Bars on roads which they themselves did not repair, but the parishes had to keep in proper condition for travel.

St CLEARS.

1839. June 15. Another party of men armed with guns, &c. went to a Toll Gate (   ) near St Clears, in Carmarthenshire, and after the discharge of several guns, set to work and countryside around. Soon many farmers got to know the curious young boy who, although he was only fourteen, was already helping his father to teach children in a little school in Lammas Street.

Some of the farmers did not pay much attention to Alcwyn. They were more interested in buying and selling in the market, or in celebrating a good bargain in an ale-house. When Alcwyn asked them questions they brushed him aside impatiently, thinking that a young lad like him had no business poking his nose into other people's affairs.

But they were not all like that. Alcwyn got quite friendly with some of the farmers and used to talk to them on market day about the news. But they nearly all treated him as a bit of a joke. They laughed at this eager young boy and teased him for being just like an old school-master already.

There was one, though, who was different. Michael Bowen, a young farmer from Trelech, did not talk down to Alcwyn or treat him like a silly boy. He was quite natural and straightforward with Alcwyn who respected him for taking him seriously, and the two of them became good friends.

3 Rebecca

One market day in November 1842 Alcwyn met Mike Bowen in the streets of Carmarthen. Mike seemed to be rather upset and wanted to talk to someone.

'What's the matter?' asked Alcwyn, in Welsh.

'Rebecca's been at it again,' answered Mike.

'Who's Rebecca? And what's she been at?' The boy was puzzled.

'Don't you remember, a few years ago at Efailwen, back in 1839? Oh no, I don't suppose you do. You'd only have been eleven then.'

'I've heard people talk about it, but I don't remember anything about a woman called Rebecca. Will you tell me the story?'

Mike was only too pleased to do so. It seemed to take his mind off something that was worrying him.

'Well,' began Mike, 'it was just about the beginning of the *lime* carting season – May time that would be. The lime is good for the land, you know, and has to be brought in wagons along the *turnpike roads*. It's a terrible business too, stopping every few miles to pay tolls at this gate or that gate. As if the lime isn't costly enough in the first place. Anyway, there was a new toll farmer on the Whitland gates, an Englishman called Thomas Bullin.'

'What's a toll farmer?' interrupted Alcwyn. 'Is he like a sheep farmer?'

'Not quite,' answered Mike. He was trying hard not to laugh at Alcwyn because it was a sensible enough question even though it sounded strange to him. 'The *turnpike trusts* 11

An artist's view of Carmarthen market in 1850

that built the roads rent out the toll gates to someone. We call him the toll farmer. He pays a fixed rent to the trust and gets what toll he can from the traffic that passes through the gates. And this Bullin makes sure he gets every penny. There used to be local men farming the gates and they would let you through free if you weren't going very far, or let you pay later if you were short of money. But not Bullin. His collectors are sharp as shears ready to fleece you of as much money as they can get. And they get into trouble if they let anyone through without paying. They're out of a job in no time at all, and Bullin will find new toll keepers with even harder hearts to take their place.

'This grasping Bullin got the Whitland trust to put up four new gates. But he'd gone too far this time. They hadn't been up a week when the gate at Efailwen was destroyed one night. It didn't make any difference to Bullin. He made sure the gate was built again. But he wasn't getting away with that. Notices were put around saying there would be a meeting "to consider the necessity of a toll gate at Efailwen". That was the phrase. It sounded very official and proper, but there was no doubt what the meeting would decide. It would be down with the gate all right. Bullin was scared when he saw the notices. So were the *magistrates*. They appointed seven *special constables* and sent them to guard the gate. Only seven, mind you. That wasn't much good. Four hundred men came along to the meeting. Some of them were afraid of being recognised so they dressed up in women's clothes and blacked their faces with coal. The special constables didn't stand a chance. They ran away as quick as they could. The crowd got to work with sledge hammers and saws. There wasn't a thing left of the gate or the gate posts and the toll house was in ruins by the time they had done.

'Well, the special constables weren't much good, so the magistrates sent off to London to ask for soldiers. Twenty-five marched over from Brecon. They came to Narberth on a Sunday morning just as people were on their way to chapel. They marched through the streets with their bayonets fixed as if they were going to charge any minute. It was a silly

This is how the 'Illustrated London News' of 1843 saw the followers of Rebecca

13

thing to do, scaring people on a Sunday morning like that. It turned a lot of respectable chapel-goers against them.

'Anyway, they weren't in Efailwen when the gate was pulled down again. Yes, the third time! Bullin's as stubborn as can be. He put the gate up again, as if nothing had happened. This third time Twm Carnabwth was in charge of pulling down the gates. He's a huge man and a powerful fighter. He wins all the prizes for fighting in the fairs, you know. I wouldn't like to take him on. He's well over six foot and broad shoulders too. Anyway he wanted to dress up in women's clothes to disguise himself. I don't know why he bothered. He'd be recognised a mile off even if he was wearing Queen Victoria's petticoat. But he insisted. The trouble was he couldn't fit into anyone's skirts. In the end someone remembered big 'Becca over at Llangolman. She's an enormous woman. Skirts like a tent. Mind you, Twm could only just squeeze into them, he's that big.

'So they hammered the gate down once again. And while they were doing it Twm was called 'Becca as a bit of a joke. But it was a good name. When my old father heard about it he went over to the family bible, all solemn as if he was in chapel. "Let me see now," he says to himself. "There's a verse in the good book as I remember. Genesis it'll be," and he turns the pages till he finds it and reads it out like he was reading the scriptures on a Sunday morning: "And they blessed Rebecca and said to her, be the mother of thousands of millions and let your children possess the gates of those which hate them."'

Mike paused as if his story was ended, but Alcwyn was still full of questions.

'What did Bullin do?' he asked. 'Did he have the gate built a fourth time?'

'He'd like to have done, I think, but the magistrates wouldn't let him. They said he couldn't have his four new gates and he'd have to make do with the old ones. I think the magistrates must have been scared. They're not usually on the side of the farmers.'

'I thought they weren't supposed to be on anyone's side.'

'Maybe they're not supposed to be,' answered Mike, smiling at what Alcwyn had said. 'But you can be sure they are. They're all *gentry* you see. Most of them don't speak Welsh and a lot of them spend half their time in London, living like kings on the money they get from rents. Being landowners it's no wonder they're hard on the tenants when they can't pay their rent.'

'Did Bullin learn his lesson then?'

'It takes more than magistrates to get anything into the skull of a man like Thomas Bullin, whose only thought is for money. Hasn't he gone and done the same thing all over again? Down in St Clears he's put up another new gate. Serve him right that Rebecca's pulled it down again.'

'Has Twm Carnabwth gone all the way over to St Clears in big 'Becca's clothes then?'

'Oh no. Twm's back to his farm and his prize fighting, I should think. It'd be someone from St Clears who played the part of Rebecca. The story of Efailwen has been told a lot round here. So they'd have called their leader 'Becca to show Bullin that they'd win just as they had before. I only hope Rebecca sticks to toll gates though, and doesn't start any other mischief.'

Alcwyn was just about to ask Mike what he meant, but Mike cut him short.

'I must be getting off home to my wife in Trelech. I'll see you again,' and he walked off looking as if he was worried about what Rebecca and her daughters might get up to next.

4 The Background

Alcwyn thought a lot about Mike's story. Somehow it didn't quite seem to make sense. He knew some of the farmers from Efailwen and from St Clears. They were respectable men even if they were not very rich and Alcwyn found it difficult to imagine them dressing up in women's clothes in order to smash the toll gates. The fishermen in Carmarthen were a rough lot. He could imagine them getting up to such tricks. But the farmers were religious men who would not go smashing things up just to save a few pennies.

That was the most puzzling thing of all. The tolls did not cost the farmers so very much. They had a hard time getting a living from the land and they had to pay out a lot of money. But the tolls were not very expensive. Alcwyn could not understand why it was the toll gates they attacked when there seemed to be so many other things to complain about.

But Mike's story was certainly true. Throughout that winter and early spring news kept coming into Carmarthen of Rebecca's adventures. There were reports in newspapers – the 'Carmarthen Journal' and the 'Welshman' as well as the Welsh language weekly papers 'Yr Haul' and 'Y Diwygiwr'. The two Welsh papers were religious and appealed to the rioters not to be violent, although 'Y Diwygiwr' obviously sympathised greatly with the farmers' problems.

There were many rumours at that time about who this mysterious lady, Rebecca, really was. Some said that 'she' was one of the gentry and came from a rich landowning family. This was a very surprising rumour because there were

not many gentry who were on the side of the farmers. There

was, in fact, a great gulf between the rich landowners and the poor farmers. They spoke different languages and worshipped in different churches. The farmers were all Welsh speaking – indeed many of them would not have known any English. But the landowners, although some of them were Welsh by birth, were often educated in England and hardly any of them took the trouble to learn Welsh. The *established church*, the Church of England, was attended by the landowners, but most of the Welsh population went to Methodist and other *non-conformist* chapels.

In those days people thought this difference of religion was very important. Nearly everybody went regularly to church or chapel and felt strongly that their own religion was the right one. Many members of the Church of England thought that the non-conformists were wicked and that young farmers only went to prayer meetings to pick up girl friends. Many non-conformists felt that the Church of England had forgotten the teachings of Jesus and was on the side of the rich and powerful instead of the humble and meek.

There were two nations in West Wales. The landowners were English speakers who spent most of their time and money in England and belonged to the Church of England. They ate well and lived in large houses. The rest of the population, mainly farmers and farm labourers, were Welsh speakers and were nearly all non-conformists. They lived in tiny hcuses and struggled to make a living from the poor land.

So it certainly seems unlikely that any of the landowners joined in the riots. But the rumours reached as far as London. The 'Illustrated London News' declared that Rebecca was 'said to be a county magistrate' and all the magistrates at that time were gentry. People also said that 'she' must be well educated since she was 'able to write her letters in Latin as well as English'. But this was imagining things.

She certainly wrote a lot of letters, though most were in Welsh or bad English and only one contains two words of Latin. They were threatening letters, sometimes addressed to her enemies like Thomas Bullin, but sometimes addressed 17 to farmers threatening to burn their houses down if they did not join in the riots.

In spite of all these stories about Rebecca, Alcwyn remembered that Mike Bowen had told him that different people took the part of Rebecca on different occasions. He realised that this must be true because there were often riots in different parts of the country on the same night, and not even a rich landowner could be in two places at once! He guessed that the part of Rebecca would usually be taken by a young farmer from the neighbourhood, men like Twm Carnabwth, or even Mike Bowen. . .

But why? It was a terrible risk to take. If the rioters were caught they would be put in prison or sent out to prison colonies in Australia. They could not be doing it just to save a small amount of money going through the toll gate.

One evening, when the children had just left the schoolroom, Alcwyn was alone with his father. He asked him why so many toll gates were being destroyed.

'Because the farmers don't like paying tolls,' said his father, scarcely looking up from the book he was studying.

'But father, they are God fearing men. Why should they take to violence just to save a few pennies?'

This time his father looked up, shut his book, and after a pause began: 'My dear Alcwyn, you have the knack of asking a good question. It is a precious gift; far better than giving an easy answer.'

And again Alcwyn's father paused for so long that Alcwyn thought he had forgotten the question. But at last he said:

'I think they do it because they know no other way to show how angry and despairing they are. They are beaten down by poverty. The rents they pay to the landlords are very high. The trouble is that there are so many people wanting a farm that at the auction sales they bid against each other and end up by offering to pay much more than they can afford. That's why there is so much fuss when a farmer takes on a second farm. There was quite a business about that in Trelech a few years ago.'

18

Alcwyn pricked up his ears. Trelech was where Mike Bowen lived.

'I believe a man called David Lewis wanted to buy a second farm. His neighbours made an *effigy* of him out of straw and took it along to his farmyard where they burnt it. They say it's a miracle his haystack didn't go up in smoke as well. I shouldn't be surprised if Rebecca starts doing something about farmers with more than one farm. That'll be the next thing after the toll gates. Though it should be the landlords they get at. They're at the root of the trouble.'

Alcwyn was worried by what his father had said, because he seemed to remember that Mike had two farms. Perhaps that's why he had been looking so worried the day he met him in Carmarthen. But his father was still talking.

'Then there's the *tithes* the farmers have to pay to the gentry.'

'But I thought tithes were paid to the church, father,' interrupted Alcwyn.

'Indeed, my boy,' said his father gently. 'And what do you know about tithes?'

'I was reading in a history book, father, that tithes were paid to priests and monks. One tenth of whatever a farmer grew – corn or vegetables or anything else – had to be given to the church.'

'That's the way it used to be, it's true. But over the years things have changed. Now a lot of the tithes find their way into the landowners' pockets. Here in Carmarthen, for instance, the tithes of St Peter's Church are worth nearly £1,000 a year. The vicar only gets £7 of that. The rest all go to a rich landowner who doesn't even live here.'

'What about the ministers of the chapels? Don't they get any of the tithes?'

'Not a penny. They have to live on the offerings they get from the people who go to their chapels. That's why we always take money to put in the plate when we go to chapel.'

Alcwyn's father sighed and, reaching for his book, he went on with his task of preparing the lessons for the next day. 19

5 The Farmers

Indeed it was true that Mike Bowen had two farms. They were small enough, only amounting to 100 acres altogether (about 40 hectares). But Mike was certainly better off than most of his neighbours. For a start he did not have to pay rent, because his father owned both Mike's farms together with two larger ones (about 600 acres or 240 hectares in all) that he farmed himself.

Most farmers in the district rented land from one of the large landowners. The average farm size in this part of Wales at that time was about 50 acres (20 hectares) which is little enough when you consider that a football pitch is about 2 acres. So an entire farm would only be the size of twenty-five football pitches. Welsh farms were usually much smaller than English farms because the Welsh used to divide a man's land up between all his sons when he died. In England the eldest son usually inherited all his father's land.

A newspaper account, written at the time, tells us that the produce of a rented farm of average size in West Wales was worth about £180 in a fairly good year. The rent would be £60. A third of your income is a large amount to spend on rent.

As well as rent, the farmer would have to pay tithes of £9. In 1836 a law had been passed to say that tithes had to be paid in cash. The law was called the Tithe Commutation Act. Before this Act a farmer could choose to pay the tithes in farm produce, which was useful in a bad year when money was scarce.

He would also have to spend £2 on church rates, road rates

and *poor rates*. The church rates were spent repairing the buildings of the Church of England and no money went to the chapels, although most of the farmers were chapel-goers. The road rates were for keeping up the back roads of the parish. Farmers still had to pay tolls on the main roads as well.

People also greatly disliked paying the poor rates. Another new Act of Parliament, the Poor Law Amendment Act of 1834, had ordered the building of *workhouses*. These were rather like prisons. Poor people who had not got enough to live on were taken away from their homes and sent to the workhouse where men, women and children were separated. All over the country people protested about this new Act and in many places they burnt down workhouses soon after they had been built. At the time of the Rebecca riots workhouses were still being built in West Wales although it was nearly ten years since the new Poor Law had been passed.

Most small farmers employed two labourers, although

The farmhouse of a poor South Wales farmer in the second half of the nineteenth century: the house was all one room

their farms were so tiny that they did not really need them. They did this because there were so many men who did not have farms of their own and they did not want their neighbours to be out of work. This would cost the farmer another £50 a year, since each labourer was paid about £25.

Lime and coal would cost the farmer another £9 a year by the time he had paid all the tolls on the way from the limekilns and the coal mines. This left him only £50 a year to live on and spend on feeding and clothing his family. This was less than £1 a week. The farm labourers would earn only half that amount.

So these farmers and their labourers had to live very poorly. One writer of the time described their food:

> For dinner you will see a small farmer have half a salt herring with potatoes and buttermilk – his family must content themselves with just a little buttermilk and potatoes. After the farmer has finished his part herring there is a scramble amongst the youngsters for bones to suck as a treat. Sometimes there would be a little skim milk cheese with oaten bread. Some better off than others had an occasional piece of bacon. Fresh meat is scarcely ever seen on the table.

But the food in the workhouse was even worse. 'The Times' newspaper compared the food in Carmarthen workhouse with the food in Carmarthen jail and found that the prisoners were better fed than the poor people who were forced to live in the workhouse. 'The Times' was very much against the new poor law. In July 1843 it published an article in which a Welsh farmer explained why the people of West Wales did not like the workhouses:

> 'It is not like England here,' he said. 'The farms are small and the farmers as well as the labourers are very poor. When the harvest is being gathered in we do not, as they do in England, have a lot of Irish and other labourers, who at the end of the harvest leave and are no longer any

trouble, but our own people only are employed as *agricultural labourers*, and they live in the parish. These people have a small cottage each to live in, and a little garden, and many of them arrive actually at almost the starvation point with their wives and children, rather than apply for *relief*, knowing that if they do so they will be dragged into the workhouse where they will be placed, themselves in one yard, their wives in another, their male children in a third, and their daughters in a fourth; and in the meanwhile their little furniture, their cottage and their garden, fall into hopeless ruin. Besides are we not ourselves better judges of those who require and deserve relief in our immediate neighbourhood than *relieving officers* who are strangers, and have neither our interests nor those of the poor at heart, but care only for their own salaries?'

(He meant that local people knew who needed help better than strangers.)

Under the old system the people of each parish had the job of looking after the poor who lived locally. They appointed unpaid officers from among themselves who gave out money, raised by the poor rate, to those they thought needed it. Some of the gentry argued that this encouraged labourers to have more children and made them lazy and careless. So they made sure that under the new law receiving relief was as unpleasant as possible. They appointed relieving officers who were not local men so that they would not be sympathetic to the poor people. These officers were paid a good salary – more than most farmers earned. They made certain that anyone who could just scrape a living did not get any relief money. No one outside the workhouse could get any relief at all.

Luckily Mike Bowen was in no danger of ending up in the workhouse. His family were a little better off than their neighbours. Even after the poor harvests of 1839 and 1840 they had just about enough to eat. But many farmers did not manage to harvest enough corn for their families to eat, let

23

alone have any left over to sell. In order to live they had to buy corn at high prices. To do this they either had to sell their animals or borrow money at high interest rates and pray that the next harvest would be better.

But 1841 also turned out to be a wet and windy year. Much of the harvest was lost and many of the farmers faced starvation. They were jealous of farmers like Mike Bowen and his father, who had a little more to eat than they did. They hardly saw their landlords, who were very much richer, because they spent most of their time in England, far away from the distress and poverty of their tenants.

In 1842 at last there was a good harvest – the best for seventeen years. But unfortunately the price of corn went down a good deal. The iron works in South Wales were not doing very well. Many workers were made redundant and returned to their poor relations in West Wales. The farmers had been relying on the iron workers and coal miners of South Wales to buy their corn, but now they could not afford it. The farmers faced the terrible difficulty that now they had at last got some produce to sell, no one would buy. Corn, barley and butter were all selling for half their usual price. Farmers who had borrowed money during the hard times could now see no way in which they could pay it back.

The poor people of West Wales, who were nearly starving in 1840 and 1841, were too feeble to fight for their rights. Without enough food they did not have the energy to protest against the many injustices they suffered. But the good harvest of 1842 put back some of the fighting spirit into them. Angry at the fall in corn prices, made poor by high rents, tithes and rates, they were resentful of every extra penny they had to spend and were jealous of anyone who was a little bit better off than they were. So the farmers got angry about the toll gates – and about their own neighbours who had more than one farm.

One evening Mike Bowen's father, an old man of seventy-seven, came down from his own farm at Plasyparcau to Gelli, the farm where Mike lived. He was very upset and brought with him a letter written in Welsh. We can imagine what it said:

I John Bowen, yn byw yn Nhrelech – Gwrandewch, Syr, gan eich bod yn ffermwr mawr gyda phedair fferm yn eich gofal! Gwyddoch ddeddf Rebecca a'i bod hi am gyfnewidio y fath drefn: tra fyddwch chwi a chynifer o ffermydd, mae llawer heb yr un. Mae eich mab mor waethed a chwi, yn perchen dwy o'ch ffermydd. Bydd fflamau yn eich 'sgubor a thân yn eich tasau gwair onid ymunith ef a ferched Rebecca. Mae Rebecca yma yn eich dysgu.

To John Bowen living at Trelech – Take notice, Sir, since you are quite a high farmer with four farms in your hands! You know the law of Rebecca that she wants to change such things, for while you have so many farms there are some who are without one. Your son is just as bad with two of your farms. Unless he joins in with the daughters of Rebecca there will be flames in your barn and fire in your hay-ricks. Rebecca is here teaching you.

6 The Water Street Gate

By the middle of May 1842, twenty gates in Carmarthenshire and Pembrokeshire had been destroyed. Most had been far out in the lonely countryside, but one raid had taken place in the town of Haverfordwest, where the rioters might easily have been caught. Rebecca was certainly growing bolder.

In the early hours of a Saturday morning towards the end of May, just about a fortnight after Alcwyn's fifteenth birthday, he was woken by the sound of guns. He was very frightened at first and drew the sheets over his head. But his curiosity overcame his fear and he crept out of bed over to the window. The shooting was coming from the direction of the Water Street toll gate only a few hundred metres away. As soon as Alcwyn opened the window he heard a shout from below:

'Get back in there. Becca's at work!'

He recognised the voice of a policeman. There were only twelve in Carmarthen altogether, so Alcwyn knew them all. He could just see the policeman now, hiding in a doorway opposite. Alcwyn decided he had better do as he was told, and he shut the window again, which was just as well because next minute he heard shots whistling past his window. He could also hear the noise of a sledge hammer thumping down on the gate and of the slates of the toll house crashing to the ground.

A little while later the shooting seemed to come nearer. Through his closed window Alcwyn saw the gang of rioters coming into Lammas Street. He noticed that the policeman had run away.

There were two men in white gowns with women's caps on their heads. From the way one of them walked, Alcwyn had the strange feeling that he recognised him. Around the two disguised men were many others with their faces blackened with coal. They were firing guns into the air and making strange noises. This curious procession seemed to parade around the town, and then suddenly everything was still again.

Alcwyn could not get back to sleep. He had seen Rebecca herself – and there was something familiar about this strange lady. Who did she remind him of? He lay for a long while trying to remember.

It was a few days later on the next market day, that he realised who he had seen playing the part of Rebecca. He was walking down Lammas Street in a crowd of people when he saw in front of him a man walking in the same way as Rebecca – and he ran after him.

'Mike!' he shouted as he caught up with the young farmer. Mike turned round quickly, looking scared.

Rebecca and her daughters breaking down a toll gate: a drawing from the 'Illustrated London News' of 1843

'Mike!' whispered Alcwyn urgently. 'Didn't I see you early Saturday morning?'

Mike looked even more scared for a minute. He glanced round nervously, then his face broke into a grin. He winked at Alcwyn and then without a word he turned round and strode off into the crowd.

Nearly fifty years later, long after Mike Bowen was dead, Alcwyn Evans, the schoolmaster and historian, wrote in his neat handwriting this account of that Saturday morning he remembered as a boy:

1843 May 27. Saturday. About one o'clock this morning Rebecca and her sister Charlotte, together with about 300 of the children, paid a visit to Water Street Gate, and in about from 15 to 20 minutes the two thick oaken posts, about 15 inches in diameter, had been sawn off close to the ground, the gate smashed to pieces, the lamp post destroyed, the glass in the windows broken and the tiled roof stripped.

About ten minutes before, the collector had been out taking toll for a cart, and he had only just returned and laid himself down in his clothes on the bed when he heard the tramp of feet and horses and a thundering noise at the gate. He got up at once and ran towards the door, but before he could reach it it was burst open against him and Rebecca and her sister came into the room. He, seeing that it would be useless to make any resistance, and that he might save himself from ill treatment, said 'Ho, Becca is here! Go on with your work! You are quite welcome!!' Becca told him not to alarm himself, as they would do no harm or injury whatever to him. He then begged her not to destroy the furniture, as it was his own. He also said that his wife and child were in bed; and that Becca might do as she liked with the gate and the toll house.

Rebecca stepped to the door to order that nothing was to be touched save the gate and the posts, and the roof of the house – that the ceiling was not to be broken for fear that the rain would come in upon the woman and child in bed.

Before they began breaking the gate, Rebecca had taken the precaution of placing about a dozen of her daughters with guns in their hands to guard the half of Water Street in which they were, and they kept firing down the other half leading into Lammas Street, so that it was almost impossible for any person to approach the gate. A drunken man who happened to hear the noise went out and called 'Hurrah, Becca!' The guards turned him back at once, saying 'Go about your business, there's a good fellow, you are not wanted. We are enough here already.' After the gate had been chopped up, the posts sawn off, the lamp and gas pipe destroyed, the windows smashed, the toll board taken down and hacked to pieces, then Rebecca told the collector that, had it not been for his politeness to them, the house itself would have been taken entirely down.

They behaved remarkably well to the toll man and frequently told him and his wife not to be alarmed, as they should not suffer the slightest injury, and at parting Becca told him not to demand tolls any more at that gate.

The people living near the gate got up and tried to look out through the windows, but they were ordered back and they could hear the *small shot* whistling past them.

The town police also were at the end of Water Street, and they could hear the small shot pattering on some of the walls close by them, so using their common sense they resolved not to venture any nearer.

When they were ready to go, Rebecca called in her guards and all left going towards Fountain Hall, amusing themselves by making the strangest possible of sounds, seeming to imitate the squeaking of pigs.

Rebecca and her sister were dressed in long, loose white gowns with women's caps on and faces blackened.

(It will do no harm to anyone living to say now that 29

'Becca' on this occasion was Michael Bowen, of Trelech, a fine tall man of about 24 years old, long ago dead.)

But although Mike had been so polite, the toll keeper did not stop collecting tolls. In fact the very same week that the gate had been destroyed a shop keeper and a miller from the village of Talog, near Trelech, were arrested for not paying tolls at the Water Street Gate.

Just after Rebecca had pulled down the gate a notice was posted on a chapel door which said in biblical Welsh:

Hyn sydd i hysbysu y bydd i feddiannau sawl a dalo yn Gate Water Street o hyn allan i gael eu llosgu, a'u bywydau i gael eu dwyn oddiarnynt yn yr amser ni thybiont.
'Becca.

This is to warn you that the goods of all persons who will henceforth pay at Water Street Gate will be burned and their lives will be taken from them at a time they do not expect.
'Becca.

The shop keeper and the miller were brought before the magistrates. They said they had been frightened by Rebecca's message. They would rather be punished by the magistrates than bring their homes and their families into danger by ignoring Rebecca's warning. As a result they were each fined £2 which was a lot of money in those days, about a month's earnings for a farm labourer.

They did not pay their fines though. At the end of the week four special constables were sent to collect the money. If the men still refused to pay the constables were told to seize their belongings. But when the constables reached the village they heard the sound of a horn and found that their way was blocked by a gang of about fifty men with blackened faces, armed with scythes and other farm tools. The constables wisely decided to go back to Carmarthen! Along the way they passed many groups of men, silently watching them.

But the magistrates were not prepared to give up. They got together a force of about thirty army pensioners. These were men who had been soldiers but had retired after completing their regular service and were only called out when they were needed. Along with three policemen, who had been sent from London, and four special constables, the pensioners marched out of Carmarthen at the very early hour of half past two the next Monday morning. But they did not catch Rebecca napping. When they were within a kilometre or two of the village of Talog they were spotted, although it was still long before dawn. A horn was blown. Guns were fired. In a short time the party was surrounded.

However, they continued with their task and went to Talog mill where they seized some boxes belonging to the miller. But they had only gone a few hundred metres with the boxes when they found their way barred by a large crowd. Their guns were taken away from them and they were marched along the road until they came to an estate belonging to the magistrate who had fined the miller. The policemen were forced to knock down the walls around the estate. But the pensioners were allowed to go home since they had not given the police any help. The policemen were back in Carmarthen by eight o'clock that morning. Their early morning raid had been a dismal failure.

This made the Government decide that they had to send troops to West Wales. The magistrates, who were all land-owners, were supposed to stop people breaking the law and behaving violently. But they never found this easy to do. In the whole of Wales only Glamorganshire had a proper police force. In the other counties unpaid constables appointed by each parish had to do the job. They were not much use since they all had other full time occupations as well. If the magistrates thought that more policemen were needed they could recruit people to be special constables. But it was not easy to find men who would do such an unpleasant job. They were not paid very much. Also they were often disliked by their neighbours. So the magistrates found that the only 31 people they could get to act as special constables were poor and unpopular. They were easily frightened by threatening letters from Rebecca and would run away pretty quickly if they thought they were in danger.

The magistrate knew this only too well and had several times begged the Home Office to send troops, but West Wales must have seemed a rather far away and unimportant part of the country to officials in London. Instead of troops only three policemen were sent. At that time London had the best police force in the country. It was called the metropolitan police force and metropolitan policemen had recently helped to control some riots in the North of England. But it is difficult to imagine three London policemen having much effect in West Wales. They certainly did not have much success in Talog!

But after what happened to the policemen in Talog the Government in London took much more notice of what was happening in West Wales. They were worried that the disturbances would spread to the factory workers in South Wales, or even in the North of England, where a lot of people were discontented and angry. They feared that Rebecca and her children might be joining up with some people called Chartists who had started riots in different parts of the country during the last few years.

The Chartists were supporters of the People's Charter, which was a *petition* to Parliament asking that every man should be given a vote. At that time only the richer people were allowed to vote in elections. The Chartists had other aims too: they were against the new Poor Law and had attacked several workhouses. (You can read about the Chartists in two other Then and There books called 'The Chartists' and 'The Chartists in Wales'.)

In 1839, the year the toll gate at Efailwen was destroyed, there was a serious Chartist riot in Newport. Some of the Chartist leaders hoped that this riot would spark off a revolution that would sweep through the country. They had supporters in most large towns – including Carmarthen,

REBECCA

AND HER

DAUGHTERS.

WELSHMEN,

You have sent me a letter commanding me to appear on WEDNESDAY night at BLAEN-NANT LANE, armed and disguised. That your object is to obtain redress for some of the grievances with which you are oppressed is evident. But this is not the way to obtain such redress. I have been, as you know, labouring for years to gain you the rights of free men, and now that I begin to see the possibility of doing some good for you, you step in, and by your violence and folly hinder me in the good work ; and instead of hastening the time when all your grievances will be at an end, your nonsensical extravagance gives an excuse to your oppressors for refusing to listen to your complaints ; and the redress you seek is further off than ever. GET ONE GRIEVANCE REDRESSED AT A TIME. The Magistrates and Trustees of the Newcastle and Carmarthen Trust have appointed **Friday the 23d instant to OVERHAUL THE GRIEVANCES CONNECTED WITH THAT TRUST.** I have been retained on the part of the Men of the Hundred of Upper Elvet to represent their interests at such Meeting. **Do you think I will neglect my duty ? Do you think it is likely I should flinch from insisting on justice being done to the people ? Or do you think that I am ignorant of the means of screwing it out from the Trustees, let them be as reluctant as they will ?** They have not been accustomed to be brought authoritatively to account. Like young colts not broken, they must be treated at first both gently and firmly. **Do you think any firmness is wanting in me ?** Why then will you do anything that will prevent my getting the bridle into their mouth ?

Do you think I can countenance or join your riotous proceedings? I tell you **No.** And what is more, though I have fought, am fighting, and will continue to fight your battles, until I can obtain perfect justice and political regeneration for you and your children, I am and will always be the first man to keep the Queen's peace, and prevent anything like rioting or

An appeal to the followers of Rebecca written by a member of the gentry in June 1843 to some farmers in his area

where Hugh Williams, a town councillor, was an active Chartist. But the expected revolution did not happen. The leaders of the riot were arrested and many people were killed when troops were sent to scatter the rioters.

This failure in Newport discouraged the Chartists in Wales. In 1842 the Chartists presented a second petition to Parliament; and there were demonstrations and strikes in favour of it in many parts of England – but not in Wales.

Although the Rebecca rioters wanted some of the same things as the Chartists, they did not have much to do with them. Most of the Chartists came from the towns. The Rebecca rioters were mainly country people. The farmers of 33

West Wales were not so worried about being allowed to vote. They were much more concerned with not starving.

But the Government was certainly afraid that the Rebecca riots might set off a new wave of demonstrations. The rioters in West Wales had taken the law into their own hands. If they were allowed to get away with doing that, then people in other parts of the country might follow their example. The Government was particularly worried that Rebecca might decide to attack the workhouses. Many people all over the country were against the new Poor Law, including the Chartists. The authorities were really afraid that if Rebecca destroyed workhouses in West Wales then the whole country would flare up into violent riots which might end up as a revolution.

The Government decided not to take any chances. On Friday 16 June 1843 they ordered that a cavalry regiment, the 4th Light Dragoons, were to ride from Cardiff to Carmarthen. The soldiers were due to arrive in Carmarthen on the following Monday morning. They were a few hours late and when they did arrive they were only just in time to prevent a disaster.

7 The Raid on Carmarthen Workhouse

Os mae dyn ydych, ac nid bachgen un ar bymtheg oed nac hen ŵr dros ddeg a thrigain, cofiwch ddod i'r Plough and Harrow ym Mwlch Newydd bore ddydd Llun nesaf, er mwyn galw ar y Maer yng Nghaerfyrddin. Dewch heb gywilydd fel ac yr ydych ac yn eich gwisg eich hunan. Os na fyddwch yno, na fydded i chwi syfrdanu pan losgith eich tŷ ym mherfedd nôs.

Hidiwch air

'Becca

If you call yourself a man, not a mere boy of sixteen nor a dodderer over seventy, then make sure that you come to the 'Plough and Harrow' in Bwlch Newydd on Monday next in the morning, to pay a little visit to the mayor in Carmarthen. Come not in disguise but without shame as you are. If you are not there you need show no surprise when your house burns down in the middle of the night.

Remember the warning of

'Becca

Every church and chapel door for miles around had a notice like this on it on Sunday morning 18 June 1843. In some churches the clerk read it out to the congregation, and the message was spread far and wide by word of mouth. One of those who was very keen to make sure there was a good turnout was the miller of Talog, no doubt thinking that the authorities would not try to take his goods again if they saw that there were many people in support of Rebecca. What 35 the miller, and the other supporters of Rebecca, did not know was that Monday 19 June was the very day that the soldiers were due to arrive in Carmarthen. If he had known that a cavalry regiment was also going to pay a visit to the mayor in Carmarthen, he might not have been quite so keen.

So, on a bright June Monday morning, farmers and farm labourers went in their hundreds and their thousands to the tiny hamlet of Bwlch Newydd, only a few miles from Carmarthen. No doubt the 'Plough and Harrow' did a lot of extra business.

In Carmarthen the mayor and magistrates were in no mood for drinking at all. There had been rumours that a big demonstration was planned and that the workhouse might be in danger. Special constables had been posted to guard it, but they were obviously of no use against a large crowd. The anxious magistrates were still waiting for the soldiers to arrive from Cardiff, wondering why they were late.

The main streets of the town, where all the shops were closed and shuttered, were lined with an expectant crowd of townspeople. Some were anxious to defend their property but most were eager to greet Rebecca and cheer her on. Among the crowd was Alcwyn Evans with two of his friends.

At ten o'clock Captain Evans, a magistrate who lived near Trelech, arrived to join the mayor and the other magistrates

The Plough and Harrow, as it looks today

in the town hall. He told them that several hundred farmers on horseback and at least a thousand on foot were gathering at Bwlch Newydd. With another magistrate, Captain Evans returned to speak to the growing crowd outside the 'Plough and Harrow'. The two gentlemen tried to persuade the farmers to go home and send a list of their grievances to the mayor. The people there certainly read out a list of grievances – they were about tolls, tithes, the poor law and church rates – but instead of going home they invited Captain Evans to lead them into Carmarthen himself. They made the usual threat – to burn his house down – if he did not agree. However Captain Evans was not to be bullied. He persuaded the farmers to leave their guns in a nearby house, and then rode quickly back to Carmarthen where messengers were sent to try to find the soldiers and tell them to hurry.

At about twelve o'clock the procession reached Carmarthen. At its head was a band, followed by at least two thousand men and women on foot. Some of them carried brooms, ready, they said, to sweep away the foundations of the toll houses and maybe the workhouse as well. Others carried banners, with slogans like:

CYFIAWNDER A CHARWYR CYFIAWNDER YDYM NI OLL
RHYDDID A GWELL LLUNIAETH
TOLL RYDD A RHYDDID

JUSTICE AND LOVERS OF JUSTICE ARE WE ALL
FREEDOM AND BETTER FOOD
FREE TOLLS AND FREEDOM

Then, mounted on a white horse, came the only disguised demonstrator to represent Rebecca. Alcwyn Evans described how he pushed to the front 'to have a peep at "Rebecca" and soon found *her*, a stalwart young person, adorned with a horse tail beard and a horse mane wig and whose bright brown eyes laughed as it were with mischief and fun, one of which winked at me as I stood gazing. I winked back in return, for I recognised 'her' name as MIKE BOWEN'.

37

Behind Mike were about three hundred farmers on horse-back. The whole noisy procession wound its way through the streets of Carmarthen past the Town Hall, where the mayor was no longer hiding, for he was off himself to look for the soldiers. Then suddenly the parade changed direction. Up the hill they went towards the workhouse. They were led there by the poor fishermen of the town who hated the work-house and were afraid they would one day have to live in it.

It was a grim, imposing building. Those at the front climbed over the high walls and opened the heavy doors to the rest of the crowd. They were welcomed by a servant girl who had ended up in the workhouse with her illegitimate child. She led them in and did a wild dance on the table as she urged the men upstairs.

But not all the people inside were so pleased at the in-vasion. The men of the workhouse were ordered out by the rioters but refused to go saying that they had no money and would only starve. In the children's section the mob seized the *matron* and threatened her with murder if she did not give up her keys. The children screamed, 'Don't kill our dear mistress!'

The master of the workhouse asked a local official, James Morse from the Stamp Office, to speak to the crowd. This he bravely agreed to do, although by now beds were being thrown out of the windows and doors were being hammered down.

Alcwyn and his friends were now in the courtyard of the workhouse, watching what was happening. As James Morse was speaking there was a disturbance at the bottom of the hill. The soldiers had arrived at last! Morse finished up by saying, 'There now, you devils. I told you so! The *dragoons* are on you.'

Alcwyn remembered clearly what happened next:

Looking downwards my friends and I saw the flashing of sunlight on a thin line of cavalry forcing their way up the hill and through the crowds. It was the reflection of sun rays from their swords and uniforms. In an instant we three rushed to a small side door opening on the road up to the Brewery; the lock was kicked off, and crossing the road, we leaped over a hedge and were safe. Scores followed us and took to flight immediately. Mike Bowen who had dressed up as Rebecca had entered the workhouse yard, but when the horsemen were coming up the hill he clapped his 'curls' in his hat, got out through the small side door and made off across the fields, leaving his horse behind him.

Mike did not stop until he had reached Trelech, more than 20 kilometres away. Fifty years later his widow still remembered his ashen face when he finally reached home.

As the soldiers rode into the crowd with their swords drawn, Thomas Morris, one of the magistrates, shouted out, 'Now my men, cut and slash away!' Immediately the commanding officer barked, 'Not one of you shall obey any man's orders but mine!'

When the soldiers reached the workhouse they closed the heavy gates. They ordered those inside to surrender. They told those outside to keep at a distance but the crowd continued to push forward. The soldiers charged, beating the crowd back with the flats of their swords. As a result three people were badly wounded. The rioters inside were arrested. Among them was the band who, like true Welsh musicians, had continued to play throughout!

Among the abandoned horses in the workhouse yard, one of the soldiers' horses fell dead from exhaustion. The soldiers had been given the wrong directions, no doubt by one of Rebecca's supporters. So when the urgent requests for help arrived from the mayor they were still some way out of Carmarthen. Although it was a very hot day the horses had covered the last 25 kilometres in an hour. Later on, another horse also died.

But two dead horses and three wounded people were light casualties indeed. The rioting could have been much more serious. If the soldiers had arrived ten minutes later the workhouse would probably have been in flames. If the commanding officer had let the soldiers cut and slash as Thomas Morris wanted them to do, the bloodshed would have been appalling. If the rioters had not been persuaded to leave their guns in Bwlch Newydd, there would have been a real battle.

As it was, both sides escaped with a good fright. The magistrates were shocked to find that so many respectable farmers had joined Rebecca in such violent activities. The Government in London was disturbed at the attack on a workhouse. This was the sort of violence that could easily spread to England. The Government felt that the riots must be stopped at all costs, even if this meant sending a lot more soldiers to West Wales.

The rioters were also frightened. They could win victories over special constables and army pensioners and even two or three metropolitan policemen. But when it came to soldiers on horseback charging at them with drawn swords – that was quite another matter. Up to this time many rioters had treated breaking down toll gates as a game. From now on the riots became much more serious and more dangerous. The rioters did a lot less dressing up and play acting and a lot more careful planning and swift action to outwit the soldiers.

Mike Bowen had had enough. After the raid on Carmarthen workhouse he stayed well clear of Rebecca's activities.

8 'The Times' Reporter

The London 'Times' printed a long account of the raid on
Carmarthen workhouse. From then on there were regular
reports in 'The Times' written by a young man called
Thomas Foster who was sent to Wales to write about the
rioting. The reports were very sympathetic to the farmers and
explained with great understanding why the riots were happening. This made Foster unpopular with the landowners
who thought that his reports encouraged further riots. But
the farmers were grateful to him for putting their case and
he managed to win the trust and help of many.

Thomas Foster was not the only person to be sent to West
Wales as a result of the Carmarthen raid. Colonel Love, who
had fought at the battle of Waterloo, was appointed to be in
command of all the troops in the area. He had already had
experience of dealing with riots. He had been in Newport
during the Chartist demonstration when twenty people were
shot by the troops. Since then he had been sent to Bradford,
in the North of England, at the time of Chartist disturbances
there.

But the narrow wooded lanes of West Wales were much
more difficult for cavalry than the streets of Bradford. So, as
well as the dragoons, Colonel Love also commanded foot soldiers, who were stationed in Carmarthen, and marines who
were based at Pembroke Dock.

In July 1843 the Government sent more troops to Colonel
Love. They also sent him two field guns. But however many
guns and soldiers he had, he still had a very difficult task.

The attacks on the toll gates happened in lonely places, far 41 away from the towns where the troops were based. So, unless the soldiers could persuade one of the rioters to tell them when and where an attack was going to take place, they had no hope of getting to the scene of a riot until it was all over. The army and police tried to tempt people to *inform* by offering large rewards – £50 and more, which was twice as much as many families lived on for a year. But although hundreds of people must have been in the know, very few came forward to tell tales.

There were many rumours, which sent the troops hurrying across country, but they all turned out to be wild goose chases. A lot of these rumours were spread on purpose to trick the soldiers. One night Colonel Love received a report that there was to be an attack on the gate at Porth-y-rhyd,

REBECCA AND THE TIMES!!!

The disturbed state of the district and the continual destruction of Gates, together with the hostile appearance of the inhabitants of Carmarthenshire, which, indeed, amounts to a revolutional movement, have induced

Edward Crompton Lloyd Hall, Esq.

TO CALL A

Public Meeting,

AT THE

TOWN HALL,

On Friday, the 14th of July, Instant,

to express his views relative to the affair in question; and also to suggest a REMEDY to the abuses that now exist in the management of the different Trusts throughout Carmarthenshire. The propriety of conferring rewards on the *patriotic* magistrates who distinguished themselves by their intrepidity and bravery at the Workhouse siege, will be taken into consideration. His address will abound with knowledge that should be in the possession of every rate payer, and it will be made amusing by his facetious delineation of those personages who made themselves *rather* too conspicuous in the execution of their duty. (to wit, Levy).

The conduct of JOHN BROWN EDMUND STACEY, Mare, will be made the subject of a searching investigation by Mr. S. TARDREW, who will deliver a deprecatory harangue on the mismanagement of corporation affairs. The expense incurred by the employment of special constables, &c. solely attributed to the incapacity of the present "constituted authorities;" and he will move that government will take no further notice of the services of Mr. S, by conferring on him the order of knighthood, (Newport Phillips to wit), as his duty has been executed in a very inefficient manner—being at the time the mob were about demolishing the Workhouse, found in a Ropewalk adjoining the town, "fervently praying for a happy release." Mr. Tardrew will handle this subject with his usual tact and coolness, making use of some shrewd and witty remarks, in a way peculiar to himself, which undoubtedly will meet the approbation of all classes.

The top part of a poster of July 1843, advertising a meeting called by a magistrate who wanted to end the riots about ten kilometres out of Carmarthen. He sent a patrol of soldiers out to guard the gate. As they passed through a village, which also had a toll gate, they heard shots fired, as if to warn people that there were soldiers about. They found nothing at Porth-y-rhyd, and waited for a while before going back to Carmarthen. On their way back they discovered that the gate they had passed through earlier had been destroyed. The rioters must have got to work on it just after the soldiers had passed through.

But Thomas Foster had much more success than Colonel Love in tracking down the supporters of Rebecca. On 20 July 1843 he actually managed to attend a secret meeting of the rioters. His report of this dangerous adventure appeared in 'The Times' a few days later:

> While I was in Llandilo last evening I obtained some information that there was to be a secret meeting of the Rebeccaites somewhere between this place and Llandovery, and, although told it would be most dangerous for me to do so, I resolved if possible to be present at it, and personally observe their proceedings. I learned that the intended meeting was to be held at a place about a mile off the main road called Cwm Ifor or Ivor's Dingle, and I walked to the spot. At that time there was only one person present, who was walking in the burial ground of the chapel of the little hamlet. As the evening closed in, however, the farmers could be seen approaching by the various paths and down the mountain sides, until at length I should say 300 persons were present. I was naturally looked upon as an object of suspicion and mistrust. A chairman was chosen and I stated fairly that I had no other object but to gain information correctly, and pledged my word of honour that I came there with no other purpose than that of reporting to my paper. The chairman then, after some objections had been made, put it to the meeting, and the show of hands decided I should be present. The proceedings of the meeting then

commenced and speeches which had been reduced to writing were read in the Welsh language. They all told of the same tale of the poverty of the people and of the grievances which they suffered. Rents, it was declared, should be lowered, the tolls altered, and the poor law abolished.

Although the farmers were very much against the new Poor Law, there were no more attacks on the workhouses. There were plenty of threats to burn the workhouses down, but they came to nothing because the workhouses were all guarded by soldiers.

But the attacks on the toll gates continued. In July and August more than thirty gates and a dozen toll houses were pulled down. On one night, 3 August 1843, as many as six gates were destroyed in different parts of the area.

Rebecca also did a lot of other things besides smashing toll gates. In the name of Rebecca all sorts of family problems were taken care of. At night time a crowd of people, led by someone playing the part of Rebecca, would take an illegitimate child to the man who was thought to be its father. Rebecca would tell him to look after the child and threaten him with punishments if he did not marry the child's mother. Unless of course he was married already; in which case Rebecca's night time visit could be very embarrassing!

Rebecca also visited men who beat their wives, and told them to stop, or else . . .

The vicar of Bangor Teify had been separated from his wife for many years. One night Rebecca appeared at the house in which his wife was living. The astonished woman was forced to come back to her husband and the couple had to promise to stay together or else there would be trouble.

The vicar of Penbryn was another Church of England clergyman who heard from Rebecca. He received a blood-curdling letter. A local farmer, who was a chapel-goer, had been unable to pay tithes. The bailiffs were sent in to seize

his goods, but he had very few possessions. His family bible,

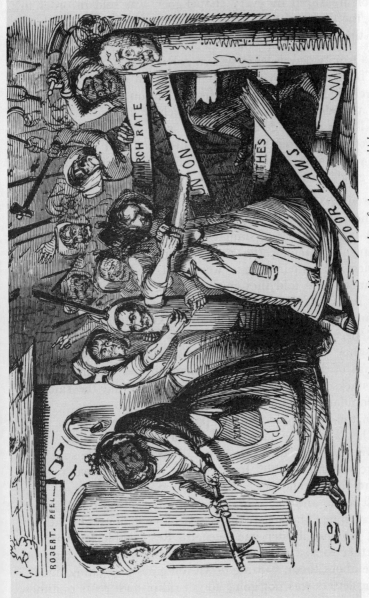

ROBERT. PEEL

RCH RATE

UNION

THES

POOR LAWS

This political cartoon from 'Punch' in 1843 shows the Rebeccaites attacking a number of grievances, which are described on the gate

45

much treasured by every chapel-goer, was sold in order to pay the vicar's tithes. Rebecca told the vicar to pay back all the tithes he had received:

> Os na wnewch fel yr wyf yn gofyn genych, nos Lun nesaf byddaf fi a rhyw nifer o'm plant yn dod i ymweled a chwi. Mi doraf ddwy o'ch aelodau, un glyn ac un fraich a rhoddaf yr hyn oll sydd genych ar dân.
>
> If you do not do as I ask you, next Monday night some of my children and I will visit you. I will break two of your limbs, one leg and one arm, and I will put all your goods on fire.

The vicar was so frightened by this letter that he asked for soldiers to be sent to guard him.

A large number of similar letters were sent to all sorts of people threatening the most violent punishments. Land-owners and their agents were told to lower their rents. Farmers were told they must not bid against each other to put rents up. And, of course, farmers with more than one farm were ordered to give up their extra farms.

Rebecca's children did not always carry out their threats, but they did punish farmers who refused to obey orders. Gangs of disguised men beat them up and set fire to their haystacks and even to their houses. They did the same to unpopular magistrates and landowners.

In the countryside no-one paid any attention to the laws of the land. The laws of Rebecca were now much more powerful. In the towns, however, the soldiers made sure that there was no trouble. In particular they took great care to guard the workhouses.

Rebecca and her children were not always violent or threatening. There were many peaceful meetings, like the one that Thomas Foster had been to. Respectable farmers got together to discuss their grievances and see what could be done about them. Cutting down toll-gates or sending threatening letters was not going to get rid of high rents or tithes or alter the Poor Law.

9 A Moorland Meeting

On 25 August 1843 a huge meeting was held on a high open moorland called Mynydd Sylen, 16 kilometres from Carmarthen. About 3,000 people came to the meeting, among them an artist from the 'Illustrated London News' who drew this picture of the moorland meeting.

Although it was out in the wilds, Mynydd Sylen was a good spot to choose. It was within reach of the miners and industrial workers from the area around Swansea, as well as the farmers of Carmarthenshire and the townspeople of Carmarthen. The artist from London saw the crowd gathering:

> The assembling of the vast crowd was an interesting scene: at an early hour dark groups of miners were seen

47

in the distance. Some were observed on the heights descending the mountain, while others were slowly making their way upward, with bended form and out-stretched step. But these broken masses of human beings, occupying such different positions, were all seen directing footsteps to Mynydd Sylen, as to a common centre.

The chairman of the meeting was a magistrate from Llanelli called William Chambers. Although he was a land-owner he sympathised with the farmers. He was unpopular with many of his fellow magistrates because he had accused them of not doing their job properly. He had also protested when landowners and tithe owners had been too greedy, and he had recently agreed to reduce the rents he charged his own tenants. But he was still a magistrate and he felt it was his duty to punish the rioters if he possibly could. So he was unpopular with many of the farmers as well and came in for several night-time visits from Rebecca.

The meeting was addressed by Hugh Williams, a Chartist, who had prepared a petition to send to the Queen. Hugh Williams was a lawyer who lived near Carmarthen. He was a member of Carmarthen town council and had been very much against building the workhouse there. He had been friendly with some of the people involved in the Chartist demonstration in Newport in 1839, and had defended several Chartists in court.

Perhaps it was because Hugh Williams had supported the People's Charter that he now suggested drawing up another petition to the Queen. He read it out in English to the thou-sands gathered in front of him. It must have been difficult for them all to hear him, although he was standing on a farm cart, since they were out in the open air and, of course, they did not have any loudspeakers.

When Hugh Williams had finished, the complicated peti-tion which mentioned tolls, tithes, rents, church rates and the Poor Law, was translated sentence by sentence into Welsh.
48 It was accepted by everyone, except for one landowner.

William Chambers and Hugh Williams had both criticised the violence of Rebecca and had argued that the attacks on the toll gates only took people's minds away from more important problems like tithes and workhouses. A young farmer, who agreed with them, although he had actually played the part of Rebecca himself more than once, proposed that there should be no more violent night-time attacks. The crowd roared approval. One of the loudest shouts came from a tall, bearded labourer who had come from Monmouthshire in search of work. He was nick-named Shoni Sgubor Fawr.

Yet that very night Shoni and his friend Dai'r Cantwr, who was also out of work, went drinking in Pontyberem. When Shoni was well and truly drunk he wandered around the village in a petticoat with a gun in his hand, shouting at the top of his voice that he was Rebecca. A man called Walter Rees was brave enough to ask him why he had agreed that there should be no more night-time violence, if he was going to behave in this way. Shoni shot at him and then chased him down the street!

10 The Battle of Pontardulais

On 6 September 1843 an informer went to the police in Swansea, which was in Glamorganshire. The police force in Glamorgan was much better organised than in Carmarthenshire. Indeed it was the most efficient police force in Wales. Captain Napier was the Chief Constable. The informer was obviously tempted by the reward of £50 to tell the police what he knew. He told them that there was an attack planned for that very night. Two gates – one at Pontardulais and one at Hendy, were the targets. They were only a kilometre apart but were on either side of the boundary between Carmarthenshire and Glamorgan.

Captain Napier took six policemen and two magistrates with him and set off for the Pontardulais gate on the Glamorgan side. A party of dragoons followed them. Meanwhile William Chambers, the magistrate who had been the chairman of the meeting at Mynydd Sylen, went towards Hendy on the Carmarthenshire side, with some foot soldiers.

Both groups were anxious not to be seen. If word got out that the gates were guarded, then the riot would be called off. They did not mind about saving the gates but wanted to capture the ring leaders.

Soon after midnight, Napier heard the noise of bugles and the firing of guns. About one hundred disguised rioters, mostly on horseback, came towards the gate. The police and soldiers watched for a few minutes as the rioters set to work. It was a clear, moonlit night. Then Napier shouted to them to stop.

No-one knows who fired the first shot. It might have been

a nervous soldier or it might have been an excited rioter. But once it was fired both sides started shooting. The rioters tried to get away but seven of them were captured, including that evening's 'Rebecca'. When William Chambers heard the shooting he brought his men over from Hendy. In the dark the dragoons mistook them for rioters, but found out their mistake just in time. Miraculously no-one was killed, but 'Rebecca', a farmer's son aged twenty-four called John Hughes, was wounded in the arm and his white petticoat was spattered with blood.

The prisoners were taken to Swansea where the magistrates questioned them. Hugh Williams, the lawyer and Chartist, came to Swansea as soon as he heard what had happened to defend the prisoners.

The police had succeeded at last. Captain Napier was later awarded £500 for his part in the events at Pontardulais. But had he managed to arrest the ring leader of the whole movement or only an unlucky farmer who, like Mike Bowen before, had played the part of Rebecca once or twice out of bravado or fear?

When the story of the 'battle of Pontardulais' got round, John Hughes, or Jac Tŷ-isha, as he was nick-named, became a popular hero. But the tale also got round that William Chambers had been the one to shoot Jac, so he became very unpopular.

The arrest of Jac Tŷ-isha did not stop the violent riots. On the following Saturday, eight or nine rioters returned to Hendy and set fire to the toll-house. The toll keeper was a seventy-five-year-old woman called Sarah Williams. She ran to her neighbours to ask them to help her put out the fire, but they were too frightened to leave their houses. She ran back to the toll house hoping to save some of her furniture. The neighbours heard several shots, then a scream and the old woman staggered back to die on their doorstep.

This was Rebecca's first and only murder. The neighbours were not the only people who were frightened. The *coroner's jury* returned this verdict: 'That Sarah Williams died from an

51

effusion of blood into the chest which occasioned *suffocation*, but from which cause is to this jury unknown.' They were obviously afraid to call it what it was: the cold blooded murder of a harmless old woman.

Since a jury of local people were too frightened to tell the truth it was clear that the rioters could get away with murder. There were several criminals who took advantage of this breakdown in law and order. Among these were Shoni and his friend Dai, who were quick to realise that they could get away with all sorts of crimes in the name of Rebecca. From then on they terrorised the neighbourhood. They were quite ready to attack other people's private enemies if they were paid for it. They would also walk into farm-houses and demand food or money, threatening to burn the hay stacks if the farmer did not give them what they wanted.

Burning hay stacks was a favourite occupation of these two. They also set fire to farms belonging to William Chambers several times and turned his animals loose. They even talked about murdering Chambers since they thought he had shot Jac Tŷ-isha and they wanted revenge.

They talked even more than they burned – and they drank even more than they talked, so it is not surprising that they did not escape arrest for long. One evening towards the end of September, Shoni and Dai met in a pub near Pontyberem. After drinking a lot they rode off to pay a visit to the English manager of the nearby iron works. They had taken a dislike to him and wanted to frighten him back to England. One of the people who went with them on that visit decided to tell the police. Twenty policemen were sent out to search for them. Not surprisingly they found Dai in a public house. They soon arrested Shoni too and took them both to Carmarthen jail.

Left: A dramatic, though exaggerated, picture of the riots: a drawing which appeared in the Paris magazine 'L'Illustration' in 1843

11 The Results

After the meeting at Mynydd Sylen a number of other gatherings took place to draw up petitions to send to the Queen. On 13 September 1843 more than 2,000 people met at Llyn Llech Owen, another remote spot in the mountains between Swansea and Carmarthen. William Chambers was asked to chair the meeting again but he refused since he was very angry about the attacks on his property. Hugh Williams was the main speaker. He presented a petition that made these points:

1. The tolls were too expensive. The gates should not be too close together. Instead of having lots of different turnpike trusts there should only be one.
2. The new Poor Law of 1834 was very bad. The old way of giving relief to the poor without putting them in the workhouse, should be brought back.
3. Farmers should be allowed to pay their tithes with produce instead of money.
4. It was unfair that all the magistrates were rich landowners. Most of them could not speak Welsh.
5. Rents should not be so high.

As a result of the petitions which were sent to the Queen, and of the reports in 'The Times', the government at last decided that something must be done. They sent three important people (called a Commission of Inquiry) to find out why there had been riots in West Wales. The three *commissioners*, who were all members of Parliament, arrived in Carmarthen on 24 October and put down in writing all the complaints which people came and made to them.

Two days later the trial of Jac Tŷ-isha and four of his companions began in Cardiff. The magistrates did not hold it in Carmarthen or Swansea because they feared that no jurymen there would dare to say that a supporter of Rebecca was guilty. Even in Cardiff many farmers did not want to be on the jury because they were afraid of what might happen to them if they found the prisoners guilty. In the end the jury was made up only of townspeople.

Hugh Williams arranged for four lawyers to defend the prisoners in court. The *Attorney General*, a member of the Government, was sent down from London to be the prosecution lawyer. This shows how important the Government thought the trial was.

The trial lasted for seven weeks. In the end the jury found Jac guilty but recommended mercy because he had never done anything else wrong. But the old judge who was trying the case would not hear of mercy. He sentenced Jac to *transportation* for twenty years.

In those days many criminals were 'transported' to Australia or Tasmania, where they lived in prison colonies for a while before being allowed to settle outside the prisons. Jac was sent to Tasmania, where he spent ten years in prison. When he was released he decided to stay in Tasmania where he married and had children. He remained there until he died at the age of eighty. Two of his fellow prisoners were sentenced to seven years transportation and the other two were let off. Thomas Foster, 'The Times' reporter, thought that the punishments were far too severe. Some people sent in a petition asking for mercy, but it did no good. The three unlucky rioters who were no more to blame than hundreds of others were sent to a London prison to wait for a ship to take them away to the other side of the world, far from their homes and families.

Meanwhile the commissioners moved around all over West Wales. People held many meetings to make lists of their grievances. These were then given to the commissioners who later put them all into their report.

There were no more attacks on toll gates in the district around Carmarthen. There were now 150 metropolitan policemen and nearly 2,000 soldiers in the area, 'enough to conquer the country, let alone keep it in order' as the Home Secretary wrote to the Prime Minister. Instead of keeping the soldiers together in the main towns they were now split up into small units which were sent to towns and villages all over West Wales.

But rioters still destroyed toll gates in one or two other places. In Rhayader in Radnorshire there were a number of riots and there was trouble in the district around Cardiff. There was even a toll gate destroyed in Somerset.

Just after Christmas Shoni and Dai were brought to trial in Carmarthen along with thirty-nine other prisoners. There were many charges against Shoni but it was difficult to persuade anyone to stand up in court to accuse him. In the end Walter Rees, the man who Shoni had shot at and chased in Pontyberem, was paid £20 in order to give evidence against Shoni. Dai was tried for destroying a toll gate. They were both found guilty. Shoni was sentenced to transportation for life and Dai to transportation for twenty years. They left the court laughing.

Shoni and Dai were taken to London where they met up with Jac Tŷ-isha and his companions. Dai wrote a poem in Welsh, complaining about what had happened to him. In February 1844 they sailed for Tasmania and never returned.

The commissioners published their Report in March 1844. They said:

1. That the toll system should be reformed so that the farmers would not have to pay so many tolls.

2. That the magistrates should not take sides against the poor and that more magistrates should be able to speak Welsh.

3. That the tithes were too high and that the landowners should put their rents down.

4. That the workhouse system should continue, but they realised that there were not enough workhouses for the

large number of poor people in West Wales at that time.

Altogether the commissioners showed they were on the farmers' side, but they did not make many detailed suggestions for improvements, except as far as the tolls were concerned. The toll system was made simpler and better by an Act of Parliament passed in August 1844. So the Rebecca rioters scored a victory in their fight against the tolls. But the workhouses continued for some time to come. However people's lives in the workhouse gradually got a little better and the Poor Law was changed slightly.

The farmers had to pay tithes and church rates for many years. The Church of England was the established church in Wales right up until 1918.

In the years that followed the Rebecca riots magistrates were appointed who were not landowners and gradually the courts became fairer. More magistrates spoke Welsh, but it was over a hundred years before the Welsh language was at last made equal to English in the courts of law.

The story of Rebecca was a good one and it was told and retold many times. It was often added to when it was retold. As time went by Rebecca became a folk hero standing for the struggle of poor people against the rich and powerful – a sort of Welsh Robin Hood.

Some of the people who had taken part in the riots also became heroes. Strangely enough the three who came most often into the stories were Twm Carnabwth, Shoni Sgubor Fawr and Dai'r Cantwr. Now Twm had only taken part in the riot at Efailwen, back in 1839. He was not in any of the riots of 1843. As for Shoni and Dai, they used the petticoats of Rebecca for their own purposes. They were irresponsible criminals who took advantage of the troubles to act violently. But people thought of them as martyrs and forgot their bad deeds.

The real heroes were men like Mike Bowen and the unfortunate Jac Tŷ-isha. They were ordinary farmers who joined in the riots partly out of fear and partly because they were made angry by the huge gap between the rich and the poor.

There were also men like Hugh Williams. He wanted the farmers to stop being violent and to get their grievances heard in Parliament – in a reformed Parliament that properly represented the people. His ideas were carried on by Welshmen like Henry Richard, Tom Ellis and David Lloyd George, who became members of Parliament and tried to make life better for their fellow countrymen.

In the years that followed the farmers of West Wales gradually became better off. The factories and coal-mines of South Wales grew and employed many more men. This meant that the poor labourers and small farmers were able to get jobs in the industrial areas. The farmers who stayed behind could have larger farms and there were more towns-people to buy the food they produced.

The workers who went to South Wales took with them the stories about Rebecca. They also had to fight to improve their way of life. Indeed all over the country people went on struggling to free the poor and oppressed from the unfair demands of the landowners and industrialists. A South Wales miner wrote at a time of unrest in the 1880s:

Mae yspryd Becca yn fyw eto mewn llawer calon orthry-medig.
The spirit of Becca is still alive in many an oppressed heart.

How do we Know?

One way to find out about the Rebecca riots is to read news-paper reports of the time. Of course Thomas Foster's regular and long reports in the London 'Times' are very useful, but he did not come down to Carmarthen until June 1843. Also he was sympathetic to the farmers so he only tells one side of the story.

The 'Report of the Commission of Inquiry', published by the Government in March 1844 has all the *evidence* that was given to the Commissioners from farmers, landowners and magistrates all over West Wales. This tells us a great deal about how people lived and also gives many lists of the griev-ances of the farmers. It does not tell us what actually hap-pened during the riots, though. Also Thomas Foster thought that the Commissioners listened to the landowners too much and that not enough farmers came forward to give evidence. So this report does not give the full picture either.

There were also local weekly papers in Welsh and English, such as the 'Welshman', the 'Carmarthen Journal', 'Y Di-wygiwr' and 'Yr Haul'. Some of these were against the riots and some of them were sympathetic to the farmers.

Alcwyn Evans used a number of these newspaper accounts in the history that he wrote of the Rebecca riots. He also made use of his own memory and the memories of people that he knew. There are three copies of the history he wrote. One is in the National Library of Wales, Aberystwyth, one is in Tenby Museum and one is in Carmarthen County Museum. Some of the things that he says about himself and about Mike Bowen show what sort of people they were. 59

The details of Mike's farms and his father's can all be found in the Tithe Commutation Agreement of 1845 for the parish of Trelech. This is in the County Record Office at Carmarthen. The threatening letter to Mike's father is made up, but it is adapted from another letter written by Rebecca to a farmer with three farms. This is now in the National Library of Wales. The conversations between Alcwyn and Mike and Alcwyn and his father are made up, though nothing is said in them that does not fit in with the records we have, or with the memories of his family, who believe that Mike did not want to be a rioter.

In 1910 Henry Tobit Evans published a book about the riots called 'Rebecca and her Daughters'. He also used newspapers of the time, but unfortunately he did not always copy them correctly so his book, although it is very entertaining, is sometimes wrong.

The Home Office in London has kept large bundles of letters and documents that tell the story of the riots from the point of view of the Government. David Williams used these Home Office papers as well as newspapers and letters to write an excellent book called 'The Rebecca Riots' (University of Wales Press, 1955). He also wrote a shorter book in Welsh with Beryl Thomas called 'Helyntion Becca'.

Things to Do

1. Write the story of the riot at Efailwen in 1839. Why did it start?
2. Make a list of the real reasons why the farmers chopped down toll gates.
3. Make a pie chart of how a small farmer spent his money (see pages 20–22). Find out how much your family spends on rent (or mortgage), rates, taxes, food and clothing. Make a pie chart of that and compare the two charts.
4. Imagine you live on a small Welsh farm in the 1840s. Write about an ordinary day in your life.
5. Find out about the Chartists. What were the demands of the People's Charter?
6. What would you do if you received a letter from Rebecca like the one on page 25?
7. Write about Monday 19 June 1843 (the raid on Carmarthen workhouse) imagining you are
   (a) one of the musicians in the band
   (b) the mayor of Carmarthen
   (c) one of the soldiers
   (d) Mike Bowen's wife.
8. Find out what it was like to live in a workhouse.
9. Imagine that you are Thomas Foster going to the secret meeting at Cwm Ifor. Are you afraid? How would you persuade the farmers at the meeting to let you stay? Write your story.
10. Do you think the farmers were right to pull down the toll gates? Have a debate between those who think they were right and those who think they should not have done so.
11. Do you think Thomas Foster was biassed, that is, did he only see one side of the problem? What about newspaper reports and television news today? Do they always give

both sides of the question? Gather together reports of the same event from several different newspapers and compare them.

12. If you were a magistrate what would you do about the riots?

13. Write a petition to the Queen putting forward the grievances of the farmers.

14. Write a threatening letter from Rebecca to
    (a) Thomas Bullin
    (b) William Chambers after the battle of Pontardulais
    (c) Colonel Love.

15. Write an account of the battle of Pontardulais from the point of view of either Captain Napier or Jac Tŷ-isha.

16. Imagine you are Dai'r Cantwr, in prison in London just before going to Tasmania. Write a poem complaining about your fate.

17. Read again what the Commissioners suggested. Write down what else you think they could have suggested.

18. Are there any parts of the world where people are as poor now as the farmers of West Wales were in the 1840s? What can people in these countries do about their problems?

19. Are there any parts of this country where people have reasons for rioting? Is there anything else they can do instead?

Glossary

agricultural labourer, a farm worker

Attorney General, a lawyer who is also a member of the Government. He prosecutes in important trials

Commissioners, the men who are on the Commission of Inquiry. The three Rebecca commissioners were Thomas Frankland Lewis, Robert Clive and William Cripps

coroner's jury, twelve men who had to decide how a person met their death

dragoon, soldier

effigy, here means a figure, perhaps made of straw, of someone bad, which is to be burnt (like Guy Fawkes)

effusion, an outpouring

established church, the church that is supported by the State and is the official religion. At that time in Wales the established church was the Church of England

estate, land belonging to a rich landowner, often surrounded by a wall

evidence, a statement given in a court of law or to a commission

gentry, upper class people, landowners and their families

to *inform*, to tell the police or others in authority when a criminal act was going to take place or who was responsible for organising it

lime, white powder obtained from limestone by burning it in a limekiln and used by farmers as fertilizer

magistrates, men who acted as judges in local courts. They had many other powers. For example they could give permission for new toll gates to be put up. They were not paid and they did not have to be lawyers

matron, here means a woman in charge of children

non-conformist, someone who goes to chapel and not to the Church of England

petition, a list of written requests presented to the Queen or Parliament

poor rate, a local tax to raise money to give support to the poor

relief, money or food given to poor people

relieving officers, the men who had the job of giving relief to the poor

small shot, small bullets

special constables, people who were paid to act as extra policemen when they were needed *suffocation*, death caused by not being able to breathe

tithe, a tax on land that used to be paid to the church but at this time it was often paid to landowners

toll gate, a gate put up across the road so that travellers would have to stop and pay the toll

toll house, house by the toll gate where the toll keeper lived

toll keeper, the man or woman who had the job of collecting the tolls

transportation, sending criminals to a prison colony overseas as a punishment

turnpike roads, roads that had toll gates

turnpike trusts, groups of people who borrowed money to build roads. They charged tolls in order to be able to pay the money back

West Wales, the name usually given at the time to the old counties of Cardiganshire, Carmarthenshire and Pembrokeshire. Today these form the new county of Dyfed

workhouse, a place where poor people had to live and work if they wanted to be given relief